This book is dedicated to Mrs. Johnson.

Desks on Strike
Copyright © 2023 Jennifer Jones
All copyright laws and rights reserved.
Published in the U.S.A.
For more information, email info@ninjalifehacks.tv
ISBN: 978-1-63731-764-8

Find the Desks on Strike lesson plans at ninjalifehacks.tv

We're there for students each day
as the teacher hands out tests.
We provide the perfect space for you
to put your heads down to rest.

When chairs are being shoved underneath us,
it feels like abuse from each side.
You don't even second-guess it
as we take it all in stride.

The teacher asks you to stop,
but you only listen if he begs,
as you pick on us all around
or kick the bottom of our legs.

We hobbled down the hallway
when classes ended for the day.
The students would return to class,
and they wouldn't know what to say.

They walked into their classroom
and noticed there was furniture, but less.
For every student was missing
his or her own school desk!

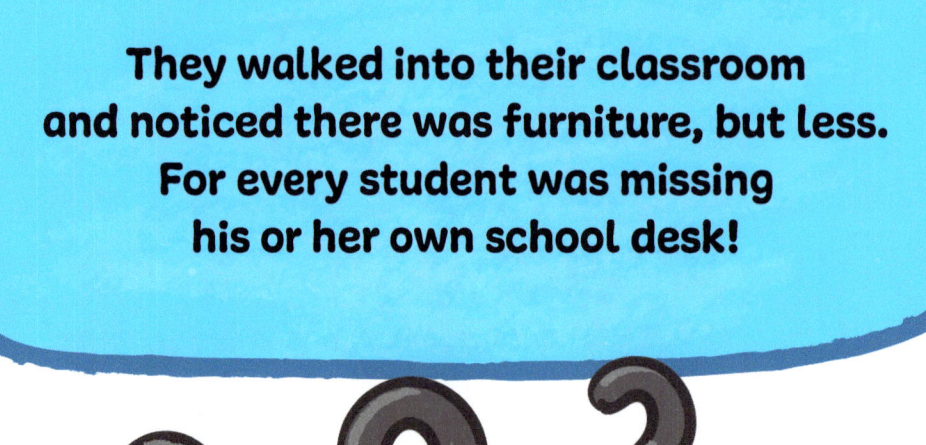

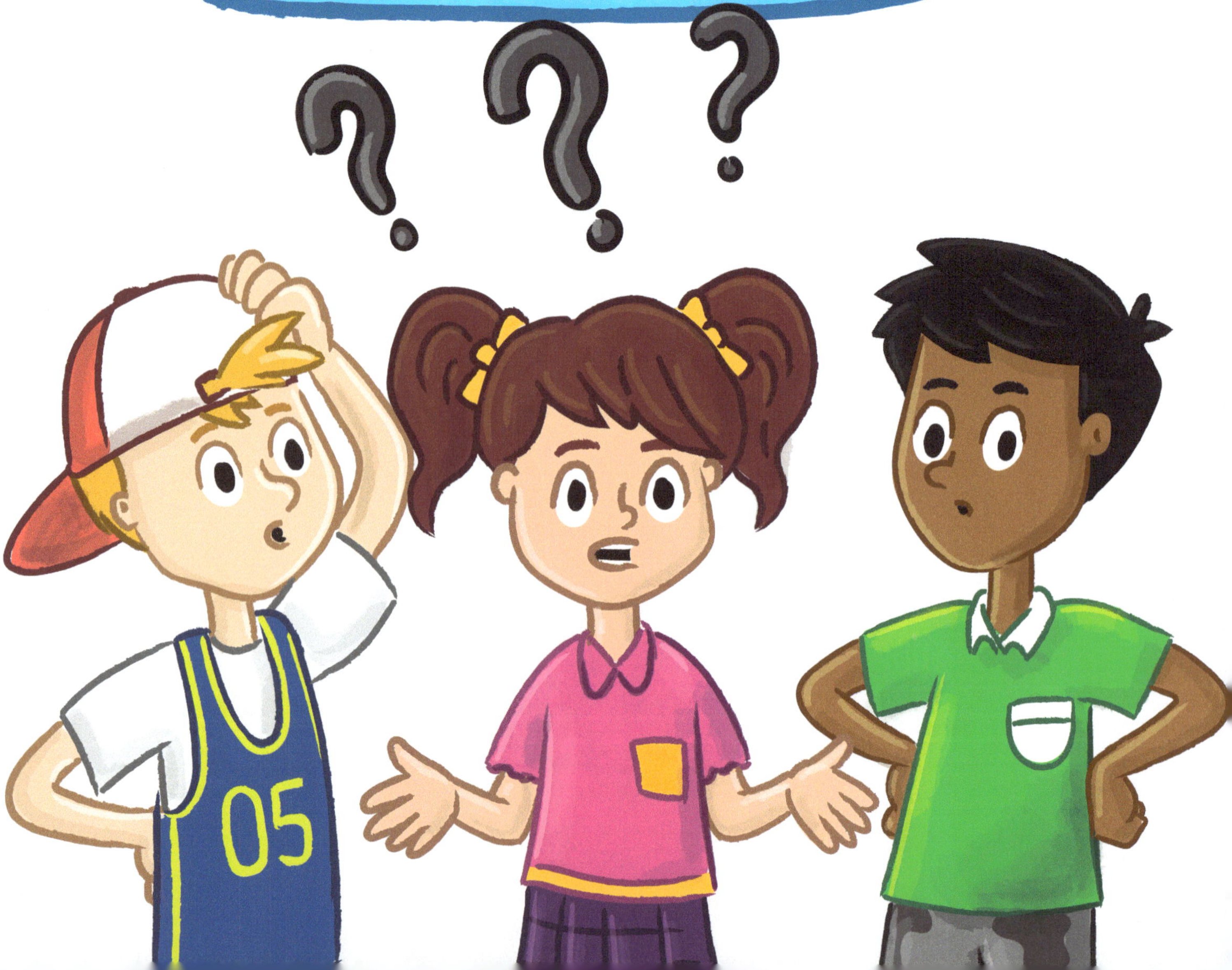

We left a note on the teacher's desk
explaining where we went
and why us desks were filled
with so much discontent.

Dear students,
We love being here for you to do your work on at school, but you treat us in ways that, well, are sort of uncool.

We want to be treated kindly,
not beaten on, colored on, or scratched.
If you promise to treat us better,
then we will happily come back.

They read our note
as they sat in a circle on the floor.
They wrote us back
and left their reply hanging on the door.

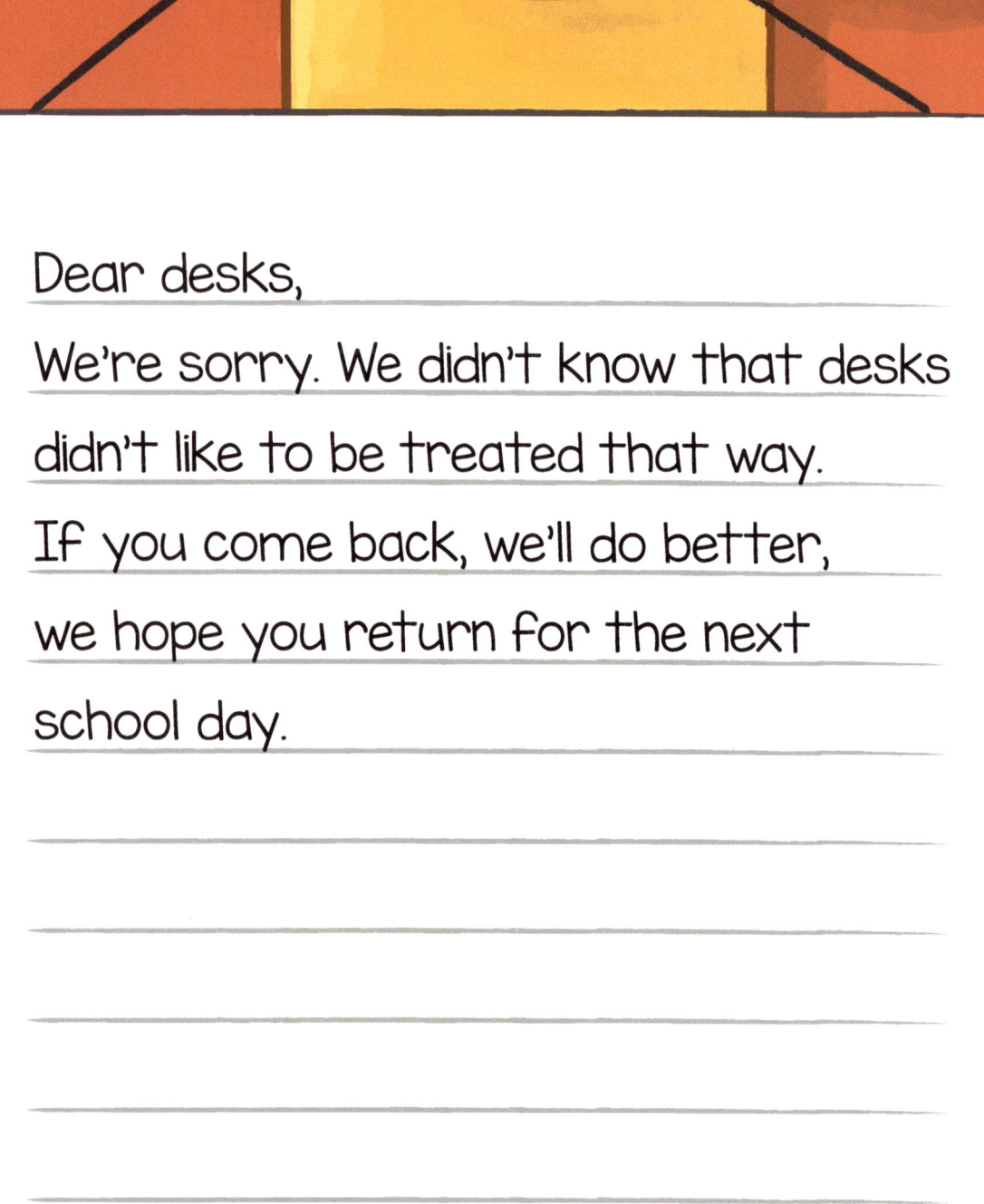

Dear desks,

We're sorry. We didn't know that desks didn't like to be treated that way. If you come back, we'll do better, we hope you return for the next school day.

www.ingramcontent.com/pod-product-compliance
Lightning Source LLC
Chambersburg PA
CBHW041524070526
44585CB00002B/69